FOR WOMEN OVER FIFTY ONLY!

Poetry of a Lifetime

by

Deborah L.E. Beauchamp

DEDICATION

To my Father.

I miss you so much.

Table of Contents

DEBUT

TOO MUCH

Right turn

to my past;

lazy days

in the warm sun;

your soft skin on mine.

Too much love

can impale the heart.

Stay with me forever

in this perfect blue sky day,

don't let the wind

take you away.

THE CASTLE

Little boys lost in their dreams;

guarding the tree house castle

from unknown foes

and fire-tongued dragons.

Time stands still

in this Neverland.

The quiet whispering of the leaves

keeps them safe;

way up there

where the wind blows free

and all little boys live forever.

PIECES OF ME

You are my life

yet…

there is a lingering…

A longing of some degree

for something that

shows who I really am.

You are everything I wanted

Yet…

It's almost like you

have stolen my identity

with your birth.

You take away pieces

of me

when you demand,

when you laugh,

when you sleep,

when you are away from me.

I hope I'll have some of me left

When you leave me.

JUSTIFY MY EXISTENCE

I offer one excuse,

only.

She died.

The soft angel haired,

sweet smelling

baby.

My baby.

I validated myself

through her

and now I find it hard to

justify my existence.

I can't stand the pain

but the sun shines

whether she's here or not

and I wish it would rain every day.

WHAT I DID FOR LOVE

The babies.

The babies.

I had two for you.

Tied the knot between us

even tighter

or so I thought.

But while I was

working like a dog,

peeling them off my hip

screaming

to the smiling daycare worker,

coming home,

tired and worn

like an old dishrag,

making a life for us

just like I saw in the glossy magazines I read

while on the toilet,

you were doing something else.

Finding a new me,

a fresh me,

someone who thought

you were the smartest person they ever met,

someone who wanted my life,

and you,

you of all people gave it away to this stranger

who gave you nothing.

ENDURE

Rain

streaks the kitchen window

blurring my memory.

The time,

it

runs like water down the drain,

as I mop

and mop

the floor.

Clean,

clean the wounds;

add another band aid.

Lock the door against the storm

as the strong winds pound.

The fight is never over

but I stay.

For them.

LEAVING

Fourteen years

I've spent here,

I could be blind

and still find my way around.

But not anymore,

it all changed,

changed that day

I found out.

The house

seemed crooked to me then.

My kitchen was lifeless,

just a dull sound from the refrigerator

and me staring out the window

not being able to move.

I never slept in our bed again

I couldn't wash the sheets clean enough.

My last night there, the house and I cried together.

MY DEAD ARM

I think I will always

remember that day

even when I'm old and

your probably dead

from running around with girls

half your age.

I will always remember your words;

that you were seeing someone else

and you were going to leave.

You had your bags already packed

and I lost my voice;

I couldn't even cry.

But I could hear;

hear the boys sobbing as you went into their rooms

and told them.

They came running out

looking at me for answers.

I had none.

We sat huddled together in the driveway

under the dim hue of the street light

watching you leave,

wondering what was happening to us.

I carry that with me always, like a dead arm.

I HAVE FLOWERS EVERYWHERE

You are an old man,

old man in a chair

but you gave me flowers everywhere.

You can't love me,

you're full of despair

but you gave me flowers everywhere.

Like a fragrant painting

that stings my eyes,

I love the flowers

of my disguise.

I have flowers, everywhere

you gave me flowers,

he gave me tears.

Nightfall is draping

over my face

but I just smell the flowers

and I know my place.

I have flowers, everywhere,

they fill up my heart

where nothing was there.

So I'll tell you

I love you,

that's all you want to hear.

At least

I have flowers

everywhere.

DISCOVERY

INSPIRATON

Inspiration is found

all around you;

in the arms of your Mother,

in the clouds,

in the touch of your baby's hand in yours,

at the water's edge.

Brilliance

is like a flash

of sunlight

on a dark, November day.

Find your muse

and listen, really listen;

you will find your calling.

FOE

An enemy
is a disquieting entity,
sucking joy
out of your unhappiness,
growing stronger
on your weakness.

A foe that has no edges
with only one intent;
to disarm you
with your own vulnerabilities.

There is no shelter,
nowhere to hide.

She lives in the open
always covering her tracks
like the wolf in sheep's clothing.
The attack is flawless
and leaves no proof
only superficial wounds
but inside;
inside
you are ripped to shreds,
doubting your sanity

       that someone like this exists

…in your family.

Sacrafiting

I have given up a lot over the years

for my writing;

friendships,

exercise,

food,

well maybe not food

but

certainly money.

Sometimes

I feel I gave up my mind almost

and any chance of a normal life

just because I bleed black ink.

My heart is too full

and my eyes only see the darkness

yet I crave writing like chocolate.

It is my confidant

quietly listening and

sustaining me

through all the bad years.

When no one else stood beside me,

I could always feel it's presence -

when I put pen to pad.

Yes, I have sacrificed

but a life without forfeit

can't conceive.

THE MONSTER IN MY LIFE

On the outside she was sweet

like maple syrup

poured over pancakes.

On the outside she was kind

like warm quilts and tea

but on the inside,

buried,

where no one could see

(except me)

boiled green evil gunge

that would

spew out of her mouth

and drip from her skin.

Her only wish,

to see you

go down.

Then she'd give you

the same hand to help you up

(if someone came by)

that she would use to push you over the cliff.

SHE WAS SUCH A BITTER OLD LADY

Bitterness eats away at me

like acid.

I try to wash it off

but it still burns.

I can't forget everything.

I can't shake it off.

Bad luck is my lady

and I have lemons on my shopping list.

EMPTY NEST

THE CLOCK

What to do now.

Can't stop the ticking of that damn clock;

it's taken my babies away,

my looks

and my thoughts – my hopes and my dreams.

                                                     If that clock would just stop.

Just give me back some of those days;

of sleepy naps with fresh babies,

morning coffee with my young husband.

Give me back

my dog and my friends

but that's not how it works

so I'll just sit here and be glad

I can still hear the ticking.

LAST BABY

You came home

bouncing

through the house,

eating through the cupboards

like a mouse.

I smelt the freshness of you

in every room.

Oh, how I've missed you,

last baby from my womb.

I can't quell my tears

knowing you will leave so soon

and your voice will be

just a memory.

Down the hall

and out the door

you'll go

to your own life.

Once I was your life.

You are still mine,

always will be

until the day I die.

THE CIRCLE

How do you let go

of the soft blond child

that grew up in the night

and awoke in the morning breeze

a young woman?

I want to lock the door

but I know you would find the key.

Your world is different now;

my world is different now

without you in it every minute.

When you come home to visit

it's like

"she's here! she's here!"

Your small shoes are at the front door,

your coat slung over the chair;

I hear your laughter like lavender in the air.

For a few precious moments

we are back together

like we started.

Oh, my precious child

I wish you could stay with me forever

but the wind is calling you

and it's how it has to be;

this circle - this damn circle.

LAST TIME

Year and years have slipped away

since I walked this path

home.

All my dreams

are there

right where I left them;

all the laughter,

all my tears,

buried there in the tall

wild grass.

The old house

proudly standing,

the only occupants

the shadows of ghosts.

The voices

come back to me,

clear as crystal memories.

My Father and my Uncle,

twins at birth, twins in death,

sitting at the picnic table;

their laughter echoing through the hot summer breeze.

I can see my brothers

chasing our black and white collie;

I loved that old dog with all my twelve-year-old heart.

I want to touch them all again

but they vanish into the fields,

their voices fading …

I sit down slowly on the blanket of grass

and take a long breath

so I will remember

the smell of summer on the farm.

As this will be

the last time

I will come home again.

SHADOWS

I never spoke about my loneliness.

It was always a whisper in my ear

and I had to push myself past it,

like paddling through the rapids.

I always got to the other side

but it was a hard, painful ride.

Always.

I carried myself like it didn't bother

ME

yet it was like a half-lit hallway

that I kept walking down, never coming to the end.

Only the silence of winter kept me sane

and I started to crave solitude and ice shadows.

Maybe I was better off isolated from humanity.

LET'S GO BACK

I wish we could go back

to when

we didn't have a care in the world,

my old friend.

I wish we could go back to then.

We used to steal away,

time barely a shadow;

just having fun was all that mattered

and then,

and then,

a black cloud rolled over the sunshine

and we couldn't see

our innocence, our joie de vivre.

GIVING CARE

HEALING MUSIC

When you were so sick,

gone from me for months,

I listened to the violins

and they cried with me,

every night

until I fell asleep.

During the morning,

I listened to horns and trumpets;

music that woke me into being

and teased a smile out of me.

In the pale of the afternoon,

piano music kissed my forehead,

wrapped me in its arms,

and soothed my weary heart.

When you finally came home,

(a miracle),

I played the music for you

in the bedroom,

the sun coming in through the windows

to listen with us.

We ate it up like good food

and got fat

and happy, oh so happy

that the we were all together one last time.

CAREGIVER WIFE

They all stay far away

up on the shore,

while I am out here

in the sea with you.

It gets lonely

and cold

and I want to be with the normal people.

But I'm not one of them anymore,

My life is an ordeal;

a conundrum,

a sacrifice and a devotion;

like a nun for her God.

Except you are human

and so am I.

I think I'm losing myself;

the sea is roaring in my ears

and the cold water is starting to feel too good.

OUR WAR

We were like soldiers

fighting life,

you and I.

All those years

struggle

upon struggle.

We fought and fought.

We would win

then we would lose;

back and forth

like a pendulum.

You always said

we had gone through too much

together

and it drove us apart;

yet we both stayed

until the last soldier was left standing.

BLURRED LINES

The lines blur

daily

between wife and caregiver;

my tears like tepid water.

There is no clear distinction

anymore

of who I am;

my titles are numerous

like a Jill of all trades.

I don't want to be your burden

so I talk softly

but inside

I'm screaming.

No one understands

the sadness, the anger

the loneliness;

like a moon without a sky.

We share the

bits of happiness

that are left on the plate

then pick up the heavy guns

and soldier on,

wishing for a cease fire.

Yet, still, in the morning light

the battle rages on

and I care

and I give

and I love.

REMEMBER

If I go before you

please don't destroy yourself,

don't wallow in the grief

like a pig in April mud.

Take the pain and dance with it;

scream it out of you.

Feel the warmth of the sun

and the tender caress of the wind.

Remember our life together

but get up

and walk into another one;

make it so.

You owe it to yourself

and me

I didn't marry a quitter;

make me proud.

CARRY ON

CARRY ON

Carry on madam, carry on.

Eat and sleep,

so easy before;

now things have to be measured in little boxes.

Coherent thoughts

are like rainbows after the storm;

so rare and yet so brilliant.

Sleep is like a raging bull

galloping across the open field

coming so close,

that you can feel the warm breath from his large nostrils

but he runs right past you, never stopping.

Eating is like a survival game.

You can only think how silent

the house is without their laughter.

How cold your bed is

without their body's warmth.

How desperately alone and scared you are

and if you will ever feel normal again.

Yet you carry on.

TRIUMPHED

Beat on your chest.

Scream

then scream again.

For you have triumphed over it.

The monster that made you not whole

has left, limping away.

He hides in the bushes now.

You know he is there

but you are not afraid anymore.

You will stand your ground

and not wave the white flag

for the war is not over yet.

CRYING WITH ME

The snow is too bright

for the dark winter night,

the wind too quiet

for the whispering trees;

crying with me,

crying with me.

I lost you years ago

and yet your ghost lingered

and I tried to be thankful

but it was never the same;

and you laid

crying with me,

crying with me.

I want to walk away

into the winter storm,

lose myself in the white screaming,

never to return.

But there are a few,

just a precious few

who might miss me too much

so I come in from the cold

cradle my face in my hands

and stay on,

and stay on.

I MISS YOU MOST IN WINTER

The whiteness of your shirt

startles me in the darkness but I don't turn on the light.

I take it from its hanger

and put it on.

I sit at the edge

of our bed

listening to the winter wind

that is crying at my window;

this is so alone

it takes my breath.

I know sleep will not come close to me,

so I drag myself around the blackened house,

stopping to look out into the white night.

I long to see you there

standing in the backyard

as the snow falls softly on the hood

of your favorite old brown parka,

as you reach out your hands for mine;

but there is nothing but the dead pallor of the snow

and the silent warmness of my breath fogging the glass.

THE STAGES

Denying it was my first hope

but that

didn't last long.

I couldn't deny reality.

I thought being angry at everyone and everything would make it all

easier,

but it only ate up all my energy.

Sadness enveloped me next, like a veil

but one day I shed it

and came to the hardest stage of all;

I accepted.

WHAT'S LEFT?

The storm is over now, only the devastation is left in its wake.

I try to clean up the mess

but I am overwhelmed with the task.

You sit there unable to help me,

crying like a child who has lost its Mother.

Agonizing tears so painful I have to look away for fear they

will drown me.

All we have left is hope.

Hope that we can rise above this.

Hope that we can salvage some of our lives.

Hope that love will see us through.

So today we feel the hot wave of life;

enjoying what we have

instead

of remembering what was taken away.

SILENT WORDS (aphasia)

Your mouth opens

but words don't pour out

only grunts of air.

Words and meanings are jumbled inside your head

like loose marbles on the floor.

I try to pick them up

but they fall through my fingers

like frozen tears.

The silence in your world

is slowly strangling you.

Robbing you of your existence,

and your identity;

making you invisible.

Nobody sees what they can't hear.

MY DAY, EVERY DAY

My brain won't stop

my eyes from crying,

my mind from churning it all up again,

like dust on a gravel road

in the middle of a dry summer afternoon.

I wonder if everyone

feels the paranoia

every day

or the fear

or the hate?

It's exhausting

and yet

familiar,

comfortingly familiar.

Deep breaths,

deep thoughts;

wipe away the tears,

turn up the volume of my laughter

on with another day.

THAT MOMENT

I always wanted to paint;

black splashed on white canvas,

dull greens and blues,

a shock of red.

I always wanted to paint you

(sitting on your tractor,

the spring storm closing around you)

so I would have the memory of that moment

even if it faded in my brain.

But the paint brush in my hand is mute.

All I have are words.

They will have to dance on the page

and sing to me. Make me always remember.

MY HOBBY

She told me

writing was just a hobby

and I should think of more

lucrative things to put all my effort into.

But how can 'just a hobby'

make me cry when I

see the words bleeding

on the white page.

Would a hobby be my therapist

through my Father's death?

And how could, just a hobby,

make me feel smart,

proud, humbled,

and in awe, all in one moment?

I smile and tell her -

Yes, my writing is just a hobby.

No one has to know,

it's really my best friend.

END OF SEASON

Summer is leaving us,

I can feel its imminent death

in the air.

I wait patiently for the long shadows,

the burial colors,

the quiet of a gray breeze

and the ample moon

to whisper sweet nothings in my ear.

I can't supress my happiness

for the cold darkness

to sweep over me

like a shroud

as I sit with only

the lamp light

and my precious thoughts.

LAST DAYS

LAST DAYS

In the last days of summer

I remember the smell of the water

and the grit of the sand

in my shoe.

I remember you sitting up in your chair

on the beach,

your books beside you

and your thermos of tea.

You couldn't eat anymore

but you could still read

and that seemed to fill you up,

enough.

I thought I saw you smile

one last time

as I did a little dance for you

in the moonlight

like I always use to do when I was young

and you knew that you were my Mother.

The summer has come to an end

and your spirit is blowing to the sea,

away from me now; these were our last days.

COME CLOSER MEMORY

Come closer memory,

so I may see the farm fields again

covered with winter's white blanket.

Come closer memory,

so I may feel the sharpness of the clean white air

slapping my cheeks bright red.

Come clearer memory,

so that I may hear the voices of us as children,

shrieking down the hill on our sleds.

Come clearer memory,

so I may look up that hill, one more time

and see my Father

beckoning me to come home.

Come slowly memory

before you fade away…

SHE WILL FORGET

They took her to her new home.

Strangers,

more and more strangers.

But it's ok,

she will forget, they tell themselves.

This person

that once was someone's Mother,

someone's wife,

someone's daughter;

it's all forgotten.

Today becomes tomorrow

and the circle goes around.

She doesn't even know her name.

The circus has come to town.

It's a party;

so glad you came she laughs.

Blissfully unaware.

CARICATURE

Days blend into each other

like paint on a canvas

and today

she sits like a cat

in the window seat,

lapping up the winter sun

trying to remember

what she was supposed to do

as her eyelids grow heavy

and close off the world.

YOUR INFIRMITY

I wanted to cry for you

but I couldn't;

I felt nothing.

Whether you lived or died

I had no control over the outcome.

And maybe,

I thought,

it would be better for you

if life ended.

Ended your suffering

and the loneliness between us

that sickness brings.

I was caught in the net

with you

even though I could swim

and I'll always wonder if those lost years

would have been my best.

FIRE

My life is on fire;

calm waters lap the shore.

My life is on fire;

water everywhere

but not a drop for me.

I can only sit back and watch the moon

and the dark blueness of the night for comfort.

I can only watch it all burn

and maybe it should,

should be the end.

I tried so hard to keep it together

but I can't anymore.

The joy of life is overshadowed

by the deep, deep, sadness of knowing its over.

He has lost his mind now

and we watch the burning house

together hand in hand.

ALWAYS CLOSE

I've come close to death,

felt its smooth coolness on my skin,

tasted the salt and the sour,

smelt the terror,

seen the flames

but it passed by me.

A flash

and it was gone;

for now.

I walked backward all the way home.

DYING

I watch your breath.

Light.

Quick.

Stop.

Start.

I sigh in relief

as a cold shiver sends my heart racing.

Waiting

for someone to die

is like watching

waves pound the shore   and   then   it   stops.

Only your handprints in the sand

where you knelt down in surrender

are left.

And me.

EXPIRED

Your death came

like

a black wave in the night;

swallowing you up. Whole.

I watch the shoreline

still

for a sighting.

Even in the moonlight

I wait for you.

I can't grasp the finality

that you simply

no longer exist.

Like a puff of smoke

and you're gone.

Ghosts and spirits are the only connection.

Hands on the Ouija board.

THE DOOR

The door was closed

like a dark force

to be reckoned with.

Heavy.

Too heavy to open.

I knew what was in the room

it protected.

Pain.

Pain and loss.

An open casket.

My Father's.

GHOSTS IN THE WOODS

Branches bundled

like someone

had a hand in it,

deep in the woods

in the middle of the night.

No footprints

in the soft green carpet

but

white trilliums

are bent at the stem

like something

had passed through;

but there's only the wind

with me.

 I think.

MY FATHER

I know he existed,

I remember him from my reoccurring dream.

When I close my eyes

I can see him

reading at the table,

glasses sliding

down the end of his nose.

I remember the way his quiet laugh sounded.

I remember the touch of his hand

on my shoulder

and I remember

watching him

close his eyes

to the worry.

I remember him

struggling for his breath.

I remember loving him so much that it hurt.

I remember all the things I miss

about not having him here any more.

But I know he existed.

Lightning Source UK Ltd.
Milton Keynes UK
UKOW02f1908230816

281352UK00001B/161/P